WHAT EVERY

WIFE

WANTS HER

HUSBAND

TO KNOW ABOUT

SEX

WHAT EVERY WIFE WANTS HER HUSBAND TO KNOW ABOUT SEX

Clifford and Joyce Penner

THOMAS NELSON PUBLISHERS

Nashville

Library of Congress Cataloging-in-Publication Data

Penner, Clifford.
    What every wife wants her husband to know about sex / Clifford and Joyce Penner.
        p. cm.
    ISBN 0-7852-7067-1 (pbk.)
    1. Sex instruction for men. 2. Sex in marriage. 3. Husbands—Sexual behavior. 4. Wives—
Sexual behavior. I. Penner, Joyce. II. Title.
HG36.P46 1998
306.7—dc21   97-28999
                                                                                                      CIP

Printed in the United States of America.
1 2 3 4 5 6 — 03 02 01 00 99 98

Every couple can negotiate
a mutually satisfying
sexual relationship.

BRING HER A FLOWER

Negotiate your differences
so that both of you are respected
and neither is violated.

Talking about sex
is vital
to keeping
love, passion, and intimacy
alive in your sex life.

Plan couple time:
fifteen minutes per day,
one evening per week,
one day per month,
and
one weekend per quarter.

Great sex doesn't just happen, but by being intentional you can make sex fantastic.

Sex is the lubricant
of the marriage;
sex reduces the friction
and
keeps the relationship running smoothly.

To be great, sex must be good
for both.

DO THE DISHES

When sex is good,
it makes up a small
but vital portion
of a good marriage.

Love, passion, and intimacy are not about
winning or losing;
they are about how you play the game.

A man can never be sure that
what a woman enjoyed last time
will work this time.

Men are sexually simpler than women.
Men are like a stick-shift Chevy pickup—
reliable, predictable, but
often not too exciting.
Women are like a Maserati—
exhilarating when they're running, but
often in need of fine-tuning.

Women have sexual urges,
thoughts, and fantasies
just as men do.

It is always better
to keep a woman
hungry for more
than to
smother, bombard, or overwhelm her.

Because so much more
needs to happen for the woman
(physically and emotionally),
a woman may need more time.

 FOLD THE WASH

A turned-on woman is
usually a turn-on
to a man,
whereas
a turned-on man can
be a demand or pressure to a woman.

The combination of male constancy
and
ever-changing, complex femininity
can be used to
keep sex alive in marriage
rather than
cause conflict and tension.

Sexually, a woman has both
more complex body parts
and
more complex bodily responses
than a man does.

Women function on two tracks;
for a woman to be ready to
lose herself sexually,
she has to feel ready both
emotionally and physically.

Men function on one track;
when a man is physically aroused,
he is usually emotionally ready
for sex.

Sex for a woman is a
total body and total person
experience.

 COMPLIMENT HER APPEARANCE

The man must understand, recognize, and respect
the woman's hormonal fluctuations.

Women can often feel used by men;
men rarely feel used by women.
Most men say, "Use me!"

In bed, the woman
has the lead role;
the man is the supporting actor.

Men often connect and feel loved through sex; women tend to desire sex as the consequence of feeling loved and connected.

Since the man is never truly satisfied
unless the woman is, he has to shift
his results orientation to her need
to connect in order for both to be happy.

When a husband genuinely
attends to his wife,
her heart opens to him,
and
her sexual attraction to him increases.

The more a man needs
his wife to need him sexually,
the more her desire for him
will be stifled
because he so desperately
needs to be needed.

A wife is validated by her husband's sexual interest if that is expressed through connection and affirmation rather than pursuit or expression of need.

 MAKE A RESERVATION

Here is a positive feedback system for married life:
the husband adores his wife,
his affirmation ignites her passion,
she invites him sexually, and
mutual affirmation is the result.

Both win when the woman
learns to listen to her body
and go after what she needs,
while the man listens to her
and responds to her desires.

The greater the time between sexual experiences, the wider the gap between men and women in their sexual eagerness and responsiveness.

Just as giving
your bodies to each other
to enjoy is
most delightful,
demanding rights to have the other's body
is most stifling.

The man has the key to the woman's sexuality—
affirmation!

RUN HER A BUBBLE BATH

Whether he has a problem,
she has a problem, or
there is no problem, a couple's sex
life will improve when the man is willing
to change and move in the direction of the
woman's needs.

Men often go for the short-term solution of sex
to feel loved.
Women yearn for sexual union when
they experience that their
personhood is regarded.

There is no way a husband can know
and meet the complex and diverse sexual needs
of his wife unless she guides him.

For passion in marriage,
a woman needs to be able to take;
she needs to believe she is
worthy of his affirmation
and
has the right to be intensely sexual.

To be free to give herself sexually,
a woman must be free
to make that choice.

The man is not responsible
for sex not working for the woman,
but he may be
vital to the solution.

Contrary to common belief,
men are not always
ready for sex.

 BRING HOME DINNER

It is not the responsibility
of the wife
to turn on the husband.

It is not the responsibility
of the husband
to give the wife an orgasm.

A woman is looking for
quiet confidence
in a man.

The woman
is the only authority
on what her body
needs and wants.

A woman can learn to be assertive.
A man can learn to be sensitive.

A man has no
instinctive knowledge about sex;
he has to learn
just as the woman does.

 PICK UP THE DRY CLEANING

A man
keeps his wife happy
when he makes her a lifelong priority
rather than a short-term project.

Since a woman
is likely to change
from one time to another,
telling him once
is not enough.

A prerequisite
for a woman learning
to lead sexually
is her ability to
enjoy her sexuality,
her husband's delight
in her sexuality,
and her pleasure
in his sexuality.

Manliness does not depend on
being married to a woman
who loves your body,
wants you sexually,
and responds to you
with erotic ecstasy.

Don't expect
to be the sexual expert
who will keep
your wife ravishingly
hungry for you
sexually.

The man needs to
take his cues about clitoral stimulation
from the woman
since direct clitoral stimulation
can cause more
pain than pleasure.

Checking for lubrication
is no way to tell
if a woman is ready for entry.

ENJOY HER NEW HAIRDO

Just because a man has an erection
is no indication
that he needs intercourse or ejaculation.

Pleasurable, playful touching
doesn't always need to lead
to intercourse.

There is no "right" position for sex.

To be great lovers
you don't have to shake
the house off its foundation,
rattle the china,
or make the neighborhood dogs howl.

Penis size
has nothing whatsoever
to do with
masculinity!

It is better to
name it and claim it
than
fear it and blame it.

A real man can be
romantic
and
emotional.

 MAKE THE BED

Whether a woman has an orgasm
during intercourse
or
from external stimulation
is entirely up to her.

The orgasm is a reflex response.
How or if a woman has an orgasm
says nothing
about a man's prowess.

Most women experience orgasm
from
external clitoral stimulation.

A woman loves a man
with the
slooooow hands!

The goal of simultaneous orgasm
usually causes pressure.

Anticipation, not spontaneity,
is the key to passion.

 GET UP WITH THE KIDS

The anticipation of planned sexual times together
builds quality;
the allotment of those times
increases quantity.

Sexual teasing that promises to fulfill heightens anticipation.

Sex works best
when you
work at it.

Make plans
that bring about
fulfillment of mutual dreams;
avoid pursuing
private dreams
that induce pressure or demand.

Sex is most fun
when you learn to have fun.

Learn about sex.
Don't count on
"doing what comes naturally."

A great sex life
takes a lifetime of
talking, planning, and working.

LET HER NAP

Pleasure-oriented sex,
not goal-oriented sex,
lasts a lifetime.

Demand stifles;
giving softens.

Each spouse is responsible for the
pleasure he or she is able to give
and to receive.

Each spouse is responsible
to allow the other
to find sexual fulfillment.

You are special, but so is your spouse;
relinquish your rights
and
give yourselves freely
to each other
to delight in the pleasure
of each other's body.

Since a man's need for connection
is usually not felt like a woman's,
sex works best when the man
learns to enjoy the process.

Sex is about
enjoying mutual pleasure,
not about her pleasing you
or your pleasing her.

 SHOP FOR GROCERIES

The criteria for
sexual pleasure
are positive touch
and skin-to-skin contact.

Go for higher levels
and
longer times of pleasure
rather than
arousal and release.

Mutual sexual joy and fulfillment
can be attained only as each spouse
takes responsibility
to do his or her part
and releases responsibility
to the other
for his or her part.

Learn to
go inside yourself;
listen to your body
and to your spirit.

You are responsible
to communicate
your unique needs,
idiosyncrasies, and preferences
from moment to moment.

Your spouse
cannot be expected
to know you
as well as you can
learn to know yourself.

 PLAN VALENTINE'S DAY

For the husband to love his wife
as Christ loved the church,
he offers himself,
but he allows her total freedom to
offer herself and
to receive his body
and the pleasure he has to give her.

Sexual love, passion, and intimacy
will be destroyed
if a man's self-worth
depends on his
wife's sexual interest
and
responsiveness.

When it comes to sex, slow is usually better than fast.

The man can improve his lovemaking by
touching in circles rather than
straight lines.

A man needs to keep his pace lagging
slightly behind her pace
in both activity and intensity.

Remove all unrealistic
expectations to perform.

Go for less, not more;
it will reduce demand
and keep you both hungry for more.

REMEMBER YOUR ANNIVERSARY

93

When touching sexually,
don't wear it out!

Watching and monitoring each other's
sexual responses
will create demand and interfere
with natural bodily responses.

Questions stifle;
expressions of enjoyment arouse.

In sex, you win
by not keeping
score.

Sex works best
when you get lost
in the enjoyment
of each other.

Sexual force-feeding
leads to
sexual anorexia.

CALL HER

Err on the side of
savoring too long
rather than
pursuing too soon.

You do not have to be
turned on
before you initiate sex.

Sexual initiation works best
when both are free to get things started
without putting a demand on the other.

You cannot fail
when you experiment
because there is no
predetermined outcome.

Surprises
that elicit spark
are freely given
with no demand
for response.

Change counteracts routine
and
keeps sex alive
in marriage.

Sex with the same person
over time
can grow in
passion and intensity.

 SEND HER A CARD

Talking about your sex life
without evaluation
expresses care,
creates a bond,
develops intimacy,
and sparks dreams.

The willingness to risk
is the antidote to losing passion
in marriage.

Passion will flourish
out of the expression
of a whole range
of powerful emotions.

As you are able to express
childlike intensity with adult responsibility,
you as a couple
will connect
with intensity.

Emotional and physical abandonment
with your spouse
will spark your sex life.

Kissing is the essence of passion;
keep kissing!

Couples who kiss passionately on a daily basis will have more frequent and more enjoyable sex.

VACUUM

Sexual excitement
that lasts a lifetime
does not rely on spontaneity.

Sex invigorates and rejuvenates
the body.
It doesn't weaken you.

Neither sexual capacity
nor sexual interest
need to diminish with age.

There is a strong positive link
between
strong religious beliefs
and
sexual satisfaction.

If sex is good only
when it's wrong,
it can never be great
when it's right.

There is no right number
of
times per week.

APPRECIATE HER WORK

119

During pregnancy,
sexual interest
may increase or decrease.

Share
the birth control
responsibility.

Don't always expect
the earth to move.

The capacity for fantasizing
is God-given;
the responsibility for the
content of the fantasy
is personal.

Everyone is vulnerable
to outside temptation;
guard against it.

There is so much
wasted potential within marriage.
There is so much
newness waiting to be discovered.

Secrets bind.
Have secrets
with
your spouse.

 PLAN FAMILY TIME

126

Newness excites;
keep adding newness
to your sex life.

Most couples experience
sexual problems at
some time in their marriage.

Temporary disruptions
of sexual functioning
are normal.

Persistent disruptions
of sexual functioning
will require outside intervention.

When sex is not working,
the natural flow of feelings and responses
is blocked by concern, conflict, or anxiety.

When sex isn't working,
seek help
until you discover
sexual pleasure.

Sexual interest
will not necessarily be synchronized
between a man and a woman.

DATE HER

You can counteract
sexual disinterest
by deciding
to be sexual with your spouse.

The security of commitment
brings sexual freedom;
possessiveness stifles sexual expressiveness.

As you choose
to relinquish power,
your need for power will diminish,
and
your comfort with not being
in control will grow.

Resolve your anger
before you
go to bed.

Since abuse is a violation of trust,
abuse interrupts the
natural ability
for intimacy in marriage.

Not feeling good about
yourself or your body
interferes with your ability
to enjoy sexual pleasure.

The fear of intimacy is the
fear of abandonment.

Know yourself,
share yourself,
and the comfort of closeness
with your spouse
will follow.

To move from
inhibitions to freedom,
take one small step at a time.

Poor hygiene,
lack of cleanliness, and sloppiness
are sexual turnoffs.

You can learn to
extend preorgasmic arousal
and
heighten your passion, intensity,
and sexual fulfillment.

Control of ejaculation
can be learned.

Pain interrupts pleasure;
sex is for pleasure.
Painful sex cannot be
allowed to continue.

If your wife is experiencing painful intercourse,
the pain is not in her head;
it's in her vagina.

Pain always needs to be taken seriously;
be your spouse's ally
until relief is found.

You are not a loser
and
she is not a loser
if she does not
have an orgasm.

Like everything else in life,
sex won't always be a "10."

Marriage is a license to
sexual freedom without demand;
marriage is not a license to
possess and control.

The delights of sex come from
the pleasure it brings,
the charge of the passion,
the sensations of building arousal,
the release of an orgasm,
and

the deep satisfaction that
comes from connecting
at your core with the
person you love enough
to be committed to for
a lifetime.
True passion takes work!

Other Sexual Resources by
Dr. Clifford & Joyce Penner

The Gift of Sex (Word)
A comprehensive sexual manual for married couples.

Counseling for Sexual Disorders (Word)
The professional's resource for sexual therapy.

Restoring the Pleasure (Word)
A step-by-step self-help program for couples who want to overcome sexual barriers.

52 Ways to Have Fun, Fantastic Sex (Thomas Nelson)
One creative sexual experience per week.

Getting Your Sex Life Off to a Great Start (Word)
A guide to prepare engaged and newly-married couples for a lifetime of sexual and emotional intimacy.

Men and Sex (Thomas Nelson)
A radical approach to how men can make the difference in discovering greater love, passion, and intimacy with their wives.

The Magic and Mystery of Sex
A 4-hour video series designed to help couples achieve greater fulfillment and intimacy. Couples share the joys and struggles of their sexual lives.

Penner & Penner

(626) 449-2525